CARDINALS

BACKYARD BIRDS

Lynn Stone

The Rourke Corporation, Inc.
Vero Beach, Florida 32964

PHOTO CREDITS
© Tom Vezo: title page, pages 4, 7, 8, 17; © Lynn M. Stone: cover, pages 10, 12, 18; © Tom Ulrich: pages 13, 15, 21

COVER ART:
James Spence

EDITORIAL SERVICES:
Penworthy Learning Systems

Library of Congress Cataloging-in-Publication Data

Stone, Lynn M.
   Cardinals / by Lynn M. Stone.
     p. cm. — (Backyard birds)
   Includes index
   Summary: Describes the physical characteristics, habitats, and behavior of different kinds of cardinals, including the red-capped cardinal, pyrrhuloxia, and red cardinal.
   ISBN 0-86593-472-X
   1. Northern Cardinal (Bird)—Juvenile literature. [1. Cardinals (Birds).] I. Title II. Series. Stone, Lynn M. Backyard birds.
QL696.P2438S76 1998
598.8'83—dc21
                                           98–11210
                                              CIP
                                             AC

Printed in the USA

TABLE OF CONTENTS

Cardinals   5
What Cardinals Look Like   6
Where Cardinals Live   9
The Cardinal Family   11
Cardinals in the Backyard   14
Backyard Food for Cardinals   16
Cardinal Habits   19
Cardinal Nests   20
Baby Cardinals   22
Glossary   23
Index   24

CARDINALS

The cardinal may be America's favorite bird. Seven states—Illinois, Indiana, Kentucky, North Carolina, Ohio, Virginia, and West Virginia—have made the "redbird" their state bird. The cardinal is a **mascot** (MAS kaht) for high school, college, and pro sports teams.

Cardinals are familiar birds in backyards. They often visit **feeding stations** (FEE ding STAY shunz), or birdfeeders. They like backyard evergreens, shrubs, thickets, and birdbaths, too.

The cardinal's *cheer-cheer-cheer* whistle is almost as well known as its red **plumage** (PLOO mij), or feathers.

The cardinal's bright feathers once made it a prized cage bird.

WHAT CARDINALS LOOK LIKE

You should never mistake the male cardinal for any other bird. He is bright red and has a crest. Other redbirds don't have the cardinal's crest or black trim around the beak. Cardinals are from 7 1/2 to 9 inches (19 to 23 centimeters) long.

The female cardinal wears a smaller crest than her mate. Her feathers are not as bright. She is the color of cream with red trim.

The male cardinal's red cloak and black trim make him an easy bird to know.

WHERE CARDINALS LIVE

The cardinal's **range** (RAYNJ), or living area, covers most of the United States and parts of Canada and Mexico.

Cardinals once lived only in warm places. Now cardinals live in cold places, too. Cardinals can be found from Nova Scotia and Minnesota in the north and south to Texas and Arizona. They even live in Mexico and Guatemala.

In their range, cardinals like places with brush, shrubs, and brambles.

Winter feeders have helped cardinals increase their numbers in the northern states and Canada.

THE CARDINAL FAMILY

The cardinal has two close cousins in the Americas. Five other birds, called red-capped cardinals, are related, too. None of the red-capped cardinals live in the United States or Canada.

The cardinal's closest cousin in the United States is the **pyrrhuloxia** (PIR uh LAHK see uh). The pyrrhuloxia lives in the Southwest and Mexico. The pyrrhuloxia has a crest and a song like the northern cardinal's. The male pyrrhuloxia is pink and gray, not red.

The pyrrhuloxia is the cardinal's first cousin. It lives in the Southwest.

The wide mouth of a baby cardinal makes an easy target for the bugs its parents bring to the nest.

A female cardinal, here on her nest, lacks the fire engine red color of her mate.

CARDINALS IN THE BACKYARD

Cardinals like backyards in all seasons. A yard needs the proper plants and food to keep cardinals all year.

Cardinals like bushes, such as blackberry. They like trees such as evergreens, ash, almond, and elm. Cardinals often build their nests in trees or shrubs.

In warm months, cardinals eat bugs. During cold months, they eat seeds, fruits, and berries. Cardinals like to visit winter feeding stations. There they can fill up on seeds.

Cardinals often visit backyards in pairs. It's easy to pick out the male.

BACKYARD FOOD FOR CARDINALS

You can keep cardinals at your feeder with sunflower seeds. Cardinals like oil sunflower seeds best. They also will eat striped sunflower seeds, safflower seeds, cracked corn, and millet. Some cardinals like melon seeds, bread, and peanut butter.

Cardinals mostly feed on the ground, but they will use hanging feeders.

A backyard birdbath helps cardinals. Water can be harder to find than food in winter. A birdbath with heated wires lets birds drink and bathe all winter.

Sunflower seeds at backyard birdfeeders are a wintertime favorite of hungry cardinals.

CARDINAL HABITS

The cardinal you see at your winter feeder may be the cardinal that nested in your yard. Cardinals do not **migrate** (MY grayt), or travel far. Unlike orioles and geese that migrate south in winter, cardinals stay in one place. By changing from bugs in summer to seeds in winter, they can find food all the time. Their feathers keep them warm.

Male and female cardinals often fly together. At feeders, the male sometimes brings a sunflower seed to his mate.

A cardinal fluffs its feathers to stay warm after an ice storm.

CARDINAL NESTS

Both the male and female cardinals help build a nest. The birds build their nests in leafy hedges or thickets.

Cardinals use twigs, weeds, and leaves to shape their nests, which look like bowls. They line the nests with fine grasses and hair.

Cardinal nests are built 8 feet to 30 feet (2.4 to 9 meters) above ground.

A male cardinal feeds his babies in their nest of grass.

BABY CARDINALS

A female cardinal lays three or four eggs. She keeps them warm by **incubating** (IN kyuh BAYT ing), or sitting on them, for nearly two weeks.

Like baby humans, baby cardinals are helpless at birth. They need their parents for warmth, shelter, and food.

The parents bring food to the nest for about 10 days. During that time the babies grow fast eating soft insects. The young cardinals can usually fly when they are 10 days old.

Glossary

feeding station (FEE ding STAY shun) — a place where people put food for birds; a birdfeeder

incubating (IN kyuh BAYT ing) — the act of keeping eggs warm before they hatch

mascot (MAS kaht) — a team's good luck symbol

migrate (MY grayt) — to travel to a distant place at the same time each year

plumage (PLOO mij) — the feathers on a bird

pyrrhuloxia (PIR uh LAHK see uh) — the cardinal's closest cousin in the United States

range (RAYNJ) — the entire area over which a plant or animal might be found it its natural environment

INDEX

backyard   14

beak   6

birdbath   16

bugs   14, 19

cardinals   5, 6, 9, 16, 19, 20, 22

   baby   22

   female   6, 19, 20, 22

   male   6, 19, 20

   red-capped   11

crest   6, 11

eggs   22

feathers   5, 6, 19

feeder   19

feeding station   5, 14

food   14, 19, 22

insects   22

mascot   5

nest   14, 20, 22

pyrruloxia   11

range   9

seeds   14, 19

   melon   16

   safflower   16

   sunflower   16, 19

FURTHER READING:

Find out more about Backyard Birds with these helpful books and information sites:

- Burnie, David. *Bird*. Knopf, 1988
- Cooper, Jason. *Birds, the Rourke Guide to State Symbols*. Rourke, 1997
- Mahnken, Jan. *The Backyard Bird-Lover's Guide.* Storey Communications, 1996
- Parsons, Alexandra. *Amazing Birds*. Knopf, 1990
- *Field Guide to the Birds of North America*. National Geographic, 1983
- Cornell Laboratory of Ornithology online at http://birdsource.cornell.edu
- National Audubon Society online at www.audubon.org